Vikings

The True and Surprising History of The Vikings

(The Stick Man with a Big Bum and the Viking Adventure)

Lewis Provost

Published By **Gautam Kumar**

Lewis Provost

All Rights Reserved

Vikings: The True and Surprising History of The Vikings (The Stick Man with a Big Bum and the Viking Adventure)

ISBN 978-0-9952066-1-8

No part of this guidebook shall be reproduced in any form without permission in writing from the publisher except in the case of brief quotations embodied in critical articles or reviews.

Legal & Disclaimer

The information contained in this book is not designed to replace or take the place of any form of medicine or professional medical advice. The information in this book has been provided for educational & entertainment purposes only.

The information contained in this book has been compiled from sources deemed reliable, and it is accurate to the best of the Author's knowledge; however, the Author cannot guarantee its accuracy and validity and cannot be held liable for any errors or omissions. Changes are periodically made to this book. You must consult your doctor or get professional medical advice before using any of the suggested remedies, techniques, or information in this book.

Upon using the information contained in this book, you agree to hold harmless the Author from and against any damages, costs, and expenses, including any legal fees potentially resulting from the application of any of the information provided by this guide. This disclaimer applies to any damages or injury caused by the use and application, whether directly or indirectly, of any advice or information presented, whether for breach of contract, tort, negligence, personal injury, criminal intent, or under any other cause of action.

You agree to accept all risks of using the information presented inside this book. You need to consult a professional medical practitioner in order to ensure you are both able and healthy enough to participate in this program.

Table Of Contents

Chapter 1: The Age Of Raiders 1

Chapter 2: The Legendary Ragnar Lothbrok 22

Chapter 3: Viking Age Monarchs And Leaders 37

Chapter 4: Trade And Economic Networks 54

Chapter 5: Skalds And Norse Poetry 70

Chapter 6: Maritime Heritage And Ship Burials 87

Chapter 7: Conversion To Christianity 99

Chapter 8: Viking Trade Routes And Exotic Goods 118

Chapter 9: Decline And Fragmentation . 131

Chapter 10: Revival Of Norse Culture ... 143

Chapter 1: The Age Of Raiders

The Age of Raiders marked a tumultuous and dynamic duration in statistics, spanning from the late 8th century to the early 11th century. This epoch, typically called the Viking Age, witnessed the emergence of seafaring Scandinavian warriors known as Vikings, who etched their indelible mark on the pages of records thru their formidable raids, explorations, and cultural affects.

Originating normally from the regions we now select out as Norway, Denmark, and Sweden, the Vikings were pushed through a complicated combination of things that encompassed economic, social, and political dimensions. Their societies had been characterized thru a mix of farming, fishing, and alternate, regularly restrained through the tough climatic conditions of the North. This environment forced many to turn to the sea as a way of survival, little by little evolving right right right into a penchant for exploration and adventure.

Famed for his or her iconic longships, which have been marvels of engineering and layout, Vikings were able to navigate each open seas and shallow rivers with first-rate ease. This innovation allowed them to reach a protracted way-flung lands, fostering the repute quo of change routes, in addition to facilitating their infamous raids on unsuspecting coastal settlements. The longship's shallow draft enabled them to strike all at once and retreat even more hastily, evading pursuit and securing their reputation as fearsome raiders.

Driven with the useful resource of a combination of monetary goals and a warrior ethos, Viking raids have been every opportunistic and calculated. Often targeting monasteries, cities, and wealthy settlements, they sought to accumulate treasures, slaves, and different valuable assets that might be introduced decrease lower back to their homelands. The monastic facilities of Britain and Ireland were particularly willing, as they held tremendous repositories of wealth and relics that attracted Viking interest.

The acquire of the Vikings prolonged past Europe. They voyaged to the Mediterranean, the Middle East, and on the equal time as a protracted manner as North America, demonstrating their great maritime abilties. One of the most iconic sagas of the Age of Raiders is that of Leif Erikson, who's believed to have led an excursion to Vinland, the region now known as Newfoundland, Canada, across the year 1000.

Religion accomplished a huge role in Viking society, and their ideals had been contemplated in their mythology and rituals. Odin, Thor, and Freyja were maximum of the deities worshipped through the Vikings, and their worldview became intricately woven with mind of future, honor, and the cycle of existence and loss of life. This religious framework provided every motivation and solace to the raiders, as they released into perilous trips into the unknown.

While the Vikings are frequently related to their raiding sports, their legacy transcends their fearsome recognition. They have been moreover professional consumers, establishing alternate networks that spanned from the Baltic Sea to the Mediterranean. Through the ones exchanges, they not best received valuable items however additionally absorbed elements of the cultures they encountered, most important to a wealthy cultural amalgamation.

As the Age of Raiders frequently waned, the Vikings commenced to settle in the lands that that they had as quickly as raided. The territories they colonized advanced into new societies, marked with the resource of a synthesis of Viking and nearby cultures. The Scandinavian impact on language, law, and governance persisted prolonged after the very last longship set sail on a raid, leaving an extended lasting imprint on the regions they touched.

In cease, the Age of Raiders encapsulated a superb era of exploration, conquest, and cultural interchange. The Vikings, with their longships and indomitable spirit, carved a completely unique area of interest in records, leaving a long lasting legacy that extends past their raiding reputation. This monetary damage in human facts underscores the complexity and interconnectedness of cultures, and the indelible effect that a fixed of intrepid adventurers can have at the path of civilization.

Origins and Homeland

The origins of the Vikings hint once more to the early medieval length, a time of problematic social dynamics and growing identities all through the Scandinavian area. The term "Viking" itself in all likelihood originated from the Old Norse word "víkingr," which noted a seafaring raider or explorer. The Vikings' fatherland comprised the lands that represent modern-day-day-day Norway, Denmark, and Sweden, every with wonderful geographical and cultural trends that inspired their improvement.

Geographically, the Scandinavian Peninsula, characterised through using fjords, mountains, and big expanses of forests, completed a pivotal position in shaping the Vikings' way of life. The presence of ample natural belongings which incorporates wooden and fish laid the inspiration for their economies, fostering a reliance on farming, fishing, and exchange. The harsh climate, with bloodless winters and quick growing seasons, necessitated a realistic technique to survival and aid manage, ultimately fostering a self-sufficient and hardy populace.

The Scandinavian societies that gave upward push to the Vikings were organized into clans and tribes, every with their non-public chieftains and leaders. These leaders held a characteristic of authority primarily based mostly on a aggregate of navy prowess, ancestral connections, and the capacity to dispense wealth and safety. Loyalty to these leaders became essential for keeping societal cohesion, and their exploits and successes frequently became the stuff of legend, influencing the growing Viking ethos.

The Viking homelands had been not isolated entities; they had been related by a community of waterways, facilitating alternate, communique, or maybe conflicts. The Baltic Sea, North Sea, and one in every of a type water our our bodies served as highways of exchange and conquest, allowing the Vikings to extend their effect past their borders. The Scandinavian human beings had been no longer truely remoted tribes; they were interconnected companies with shared cultural practices, languages, and religious beliefs.

The Viking Age is normally stated to have started out out across the late 8th century, marked with the aid of way of the number one recorded Viking raid at the Lindisfarne monastery in 793. While the motives of this growth are multifaceted, a aggregate of population growth, a choice for wealth and assets, and the supply of advanced shipbuilding era all performed their thing. The longships, characterized through their shallow drafts and flexible layout, epitomized the innovation of Viking shipbuilders, permitting them to navigate each open waters and shallow rivers with equal normal overall performance.

Cultural exchange come to be an intrinsic part of the Viking global. While the Vikings are regularly associated with raiding and conflict, additionally they engaged in peaceful interactions, which includes exchange and colonization. In reality, the Viking investors and settlers helped to set up connections amongst Scandinavia and super factors of Europe, together with the British Isles, France, and Russia. These interactions brought on a gradual mixing of cultural elements, influencing paintings, language, or even governance.

In essence, the origins and fatherland of the Vikings are rooted in a complex interaction of geography, lifestyle, and historic conditions. The harsh however fertile lands of Scandinavia solid a folks who possessed every the resourcefulness to thrive and the ambition to discover. The Viking Age, at the equal time as marked with the useful resource of raiding and conquest, changed into moreover described thru the exchange of thoughts and cultural mingling that original no longer only their societies but additionally the route of worldwide information. Understanding the origins of the Vikings illuminates the dynamic forces that set in motion an technology of incredible exploration and transformation.

Gods and Beliefs of the Vikings

The non secular beliefs of the Vikings offer a captivating glimpse into the worldview of this ancient Scandinavian manner of life. Central to their non secular device have been a pantheon of gods and goddesses, every embodying top notch characteristics and governing unique components of life. These deities have been woven into the cloth of everyday lifestyles, influencing not best the Vikings' belief of the herbal worldwide but also their actions and picks.

At the coronary coronary heart of Viking non secular beliefs stood Odin, the All-Father and leader of the gods. Odin became authentic as a practical and powerful determine, related to expertise, poetry, and conflict. He grow to be regularly depicted as a wanderer, roaming the cosmos searching out attention and data. Odin's quest for knowledge led him to sacrifice one among his eyes at the Well of Urd, gaining the present of foresight in go returned. His ravens, Huginn (Thought) and Muninn (Memory), symbolized his insatiable hunger for expertise and his attention of all that transpired in the global.

Thor, the thunder god, end up some other prominent figure in Viking mythology. As a protector of the gods and humanity, Thor's mighty hammer, Mjolnir, changed into emblematic of his electricity and functionality to summon thunder and lightning. His function in preventing giants and forces of chaos made him a cherished and revered deity, and his exploits have been celebrated in masses of myths and memories.

Freyja, the goddess of love, fertility, and magic, occupied a huge vicinity within the pantheon. She changed into related to beauty, sensuality, and the cycles of existence. Freyja's possession of the legendary necklace Brisingamen, received through a % with dwarves, showcased her appeal and her connection to each human and divine geographical regions. Additionally, she presided over the afterlife realm of Folkvangr, wherein half of of of the fallen warriors have been stated to are living after death.

Loki, the form-transferring trickster, added complexity to the Norse pantheon. Often inflicting mischief and chaos, Loki's unpredictable nature delivered each enjoyment and worrying conditions to the gods. He become accountable for engineering numerous situations that delivered approximately mythological activities, which encompass the introduction of Thor's hammer and the binding of the wolf Fenrir. While Loki's antics delivered about turmoil, he additionally performed a position in bringing about crucial changes and occasions within the divine narrative.

The perception in an afterlife end up important to Viking spiritual concept.

Valhalla, the grand hall of Odin, modified into reserved for brave warriors who died in fight. These decided on warriors, the Einherjar, had been given the promise of feasting and camaraderie in education for Ragnarok, the final cosmic struggle among the gods and the forces of chaos. Folkvangr, overseen thru Freyja, welcomed half of of of the fallen warriors, emphasizing the idea of an honorable surrender as a defining problem of Viking way of life.

Rituals and ceremonies have been a massive a part of Viking non secular existence. Blóts, or sacrificial offerings, were made to the gods to are looking for their choice and benefits. These rituals frequently came about at critical junctures which includes solstices and equinoxes, in addition to at some stage in moments of transition like births, marriages, and deaths. The Vikings believed that their interactions with the gods were reciprocal, and services have been a manner to preserve harmony and balance inside the cosmos.

In give up, the gods and beliefs of the Vikings lengthy-established a complex tapestry that interwove with their each day lives and cultural identification. The Norse pantheon, populated with the useful useful resource of effective and multifaceted deities, reflected the Vikings' information of the arena round them and their area inside it. These ideals now not most effective provided consolation and steering however additionally stimulated a revel in of braveness and adventure, shaping the movements of the Vikings as they navigated the annoying situations in their time. The exploration of Viking spirituality famous the intensity in their way of life and the profound connection they felt with the divine forces that dominated their lives.

Central to the Viking Age's legacy have been the long-lasting longships, vessels that now not high-quality enabled their legendary raids however moreover exemplified the technological prowess and maritime innovation of the Scandinavian seafarers. These clean and flexible ships have been designed to navigate the treacherous waters of the North Atlantic, providing the Vikings incredible mobility and strategic benefit of their explorations and conquests.

The layout of the longship changed into a testament to the Vikings' deep data of shipbuilding and their functionality to conform to the unique demanding situations of their surroundings. These ships featured a shallow draft, permitting them to sail in each open seas and shallow rivers, granting the Vikings get admission to to territories far beyond their homelands. The keel, a great structural detail, became often made from a single all righttree, making sure stability and durability in the route of lengthy journeys.

The longship's modern-day-day clinker-constructed creation technique concerned overlapping planks that have been fixed together the usage of iron rivets. This method not best furnished strength but additionally flexibility, permitting the ship to face as much as the rigors of ocean adventure, which incorporates waves and strong currents. The planks have been tightly equipped, decreasing drag and growing the supply's speed, vital for every raiding and exploration.

The easy profile of the longship featured a prow decorated with difficult carvings, regularly depicting fearsome creatures or mythological symbols. This decorative element now not high-quality showcased the Vikings' artistic abilities however moreover served a practical motive thru intimidating foes and affirming the supply's fame as a vessel of power. The stern of the deliver changed into further vital, housing the steering oar and supplying a vantage issue for navigation and verbal exchange.

The longships' sail configurations were designed for maximum overall overall performance in severa wind situations. Square sails have been used for downwind sailing, while triangular or lateen sails furnished better control whilst sailing into the wind. This versatility allowed the Vikings to adapt to changing weather conditions, a vital expertise for his or her prolonged journeys and strategic maneuvering.

Navigation became an complex aggregate of practical understanding and celestial remark. The Vikings trusted landmarks, coastal capabilities, and navigational markers to traverse diagnosed routes. In uncharted waters, they employed a aggregate of useless reckoning and celestial navigation, the usage of the positions of the sun, stars, or maybe the flight types of birds to decide their path. The astrolabe, an historic tool used to degree the altitude of celestial our our bodies, in all likelihood aided their observations.

The Vikings' wonderful seamanship extended to their functionality to adopt transoceanic voyages. Their voyages to locations which consist of Iceland, Greenland, or perhaps North America stand as testomony to their navigational expertise. The sagas, historic narratives that blend reality and mythology, offer debts of these trips, highlighting the traumatic situations, discoveries, and encounters that characterized those ambitious explorations.

In a global without current navigational equipment, the longships' achievement trusted the collective information and competencies of the enterprise. The Vikings' navigation required a keen information of the natural worldwide, an capability to interpret the nuances of the ocean and the sky, and the courage to project into the unknown. It have grow to be a testament to their indomitable spirit, their connection with their surroundings, and their mastery of knowledge that allowed them to embark on trips that extended the regarded boundaries of their worldwide.

In final, the longships and navigation techniques of the Vikings constitute a great fusion of engineering, ingenuity, and navigational prowess. These vessels epitomized the Vikings' prowess at the immoderate seas and achieved a pivotal role in shaping their records, allowing them to discover, alternate, and depart an indelible mark on the tapestry of global civilization. The legacy of the longships stands as a testomony to the Vikings' potential to harness their surroundings to gain fantastic feats of exploration and conquest.

Chapter 2: The Legendary Ragnar Lothbrok

In the tapestry of Viking records, few figures loom as large as Ragnar Lothbrok, a legendary hero whose exploits have captured the creativeness of generations. While the street among ancient fact and mythology is regularly blurred in his tale, Ragnar's legacy as an high-quality warrior, cunning strategist, and enigmatic leader stays a testomony to the complicated interaction of data and fantasy that characterizes the Viking Age.

Ragnar's origins are shrouded in thriller, with various assets supplying conflicting debts of his beginning and lineage. Some sagas propose he emerge as a ancient discern, a chieftain of Danish or Swedish descent who lived in the path of the ninth century. Others gift him as a semi-legendary decide, blending ancient elements with legendary attributes to create a larger-than-lifestyles character. Regardless of his origins, Ragnar's effect on Viking lifestyle and his function in shaping its legends are simple.

Ragnar's exploits were regularly connected to his mythical ability as a warrior and leader. The sagas portray him as a fearsome warrior who defeated formidable foes, along with the mythical serpent Jormungandr and the sizeable berserker undergo. His mastery of fight earned him the epithet "Lothbrok," that's generally interpreted as "bushy breeches" or "shaggy pants," probably referencing a one-of-a-kind garment he wore into warfare.

One of the most well-known sagas associated with Ragnar is the tale of his excursion to the East. According to the sagas, Ragnar released into a ambitious journey to the lands of the Rus, in which he sought to conquer and plunder. This day experience showcased his strategic acumen, as he hired a ruse to breach the metropolis's defenses and solid victory. While the ancient accuracy of this account is debated, it demonstrates how Ragnar's narrative blended history with imaginative storytelling.

Ragnar's saga takes a sad flip together with his eventual capture thru King Ælla of Northumbria. The mythical Blood Eagle execution, in which he become supposedly subjected to a gruesome technique of torture and dying, is often stated as one of the maximum colourful episodes in his tale. This event, while ugly and dramatic, highlights the saga's penchant for dramatizing occasions to create an enduring effect.

Ragnar's legacy extends past his personal deeds to his legendary sons, along side Ivar the Boneless, Bjorn Ironside, and Sigurd Snake-in-the-Eye. Each son inherited a percent in their father's mythic attributes, contributing to their very very own reputations as warriors and leaders. The Viking sagas are replete with testimonies of their exploits, along side battles, conquests, and complex familial dynamics.

Ragnar's have an impact on stretches some distance beyond his time, permeating Viking culture and mythology. His tale served as idea for skaldic poetry, sagas, or maybe modern-day famous way of life. The parent of Ragnar has been reimagined and adapted in severa ways, contributing to the long-lasting fascination together with his lifestyles and adventures.

In the final evaluation, the tale of Ragnar Lothbrok stands as a testomony to the interplay among ancient fact and delusion in Viking information. His legacy, whether or no longer as a ancient chieftain or a larger-than-life legendary hero, continues to captivate audiences and inspire storytellers. Whether one views him as a mortal warrior or a semi-divine figure, Ragnar's tale exemplifies the complicated combination of records and legend that characterizes the Viking Age and its enduring effect on human creativeness.

Norse Mythology and Cosmology

At the coronary coronary coronary heart of Viking way of existence and worldview lay a rich tapestry of myths and cosmological ideals that provided insights into the character of existence, the roles of gods and mortals, and the interconnectedness of all subjects. Norse mythology, a complicated net of narratives, gods, and nation-states, furnished the Vikings with a framework via which to recognize the area round them and their area internal it.

The Norse cosmos come to be divided into numerous geographical regions, each with its own wonderful attributes and population. At the middle stood Midgard, the arena of humans, which modified into surrounded with the aid of an ocean inhabited thru using the excellent serpent Jormungandr. Above Midgard lay Asgard, the home of the Aesir gods, wherein Odin, Thor, and different deities resided. Beneath Midgard lay Niflheim, a realm of ice and mist, and Muspelheim, a realm of fireside and warmth.

The Yggdrasil, the World Tree, served as a precious photograph of Norse cosmology. Its branches prolonged via the numerous geographical areas, connecting them and facilitating communication among them. The roots of Yggdrasil delved deep into the nation-states of the lifeless, revealing the hard interaction amongst existence, death, and the cycles of existence.

The gods of Norse mythology were a severa and multifaceted pantheon, every embodying unique attributes and responsibilities. Odin, the All-Father, have come to be related to records, poetry, and struggle. His quest for expertise led him to sacrifice an eye fixed constant in change for the information of the ages. Thor, the thunder god, blanketed every gods and those, wielding the effective hammer Mjolnir. Freyja, the goddess of love and fertility, modified into related to magic and the afterlife. Loki, the form-shifting trickster, often brought on chaos and mischief, highlighting the complicated ethical landscape of the mythology.

The gods have been not all-effective; they themselves had been trouble to future and the forces of destiny. The Norns, 3 female beings, determined the destinies of all beings through weaving the threads of fate. Even the gods had been no longer exempt from the inexorable march of future, as exemplified with the aid of the foretold activities of Ragnarok, the apocalyptic warfare that marked the stop of the area and the rebirth of the cosmos.

Norse mythology become handed down thru oral subculture, with skaldic poets and storytellers maintaining and improving the ones narratives. The Prose Edda and the Poetic Edda, written down inside the 13th century, offer a number of the maximum whole assets of Norse mythology, providing insights into the gods, creation myths, and the poetic gadgets used to recount the ones memories.

The mythology modified into no longer most effective a deliver of entertainment and mirrored image however moreover a method of records the place's complexities. The gods' interactions with the herbal worldwide, their struggles and triumphs, reflected the traumatic situations and mysteries of human life. The perception in future, honor, and the cyclical nature of lifestyles and lack of lifestyles underscored the significance of bravery, loyalty, and dwelling in concord with the forces of the cosmos.

In final, Norse mythology and cosmology constituted a critical trouble of Viking way of existence, shaping their worldview and influencing their moves. The tough interplay of gods, geographical regions, and fate supplied the Vikings with a lens via which they'll grapple with lifestyles's mysteries, navigate the challenges in their international, and forge a connection between the mortal and the divine. The legacy of Norse mythology continues to captivate contemporary audiences, offering a glimpse into the complex tapestry of ideals that described the Viking

Age and preserve to resonate with the human enjoy.

Exploration of New Lands

The Viking Age modified into marked by means of manner of manner of a ambitious spirit of exploration that led Scandinavian seafarers to venture a long way beyond their homelands, crossing seas and oceans to find out new lands and amplify their horizons. These intrepid voyages, fueled by means of way of a combination of monetary aspirations, interest, and a thirst for journey, left a long-lasting mark on statistics and reshaped the geographical and cultural landscape of the arena.

The Vikings' mastery of shipbuilding, navigation, and maritime era performed a pivotal characteristic in their ability to find out new lands. The iconic longships, with their shallow drafts and bendy sail configurations, allowed them to navigate both open seas and shallow rivers. This flexibility granted the Vikings access to areas which have been formerly inaccessible, permitting them to discover coastlines, rivers, and estuaries with awesome ease.

One of the maximum famend Viking expeditions changed into the colonization of Iceland. Settled within the late 9th century, Iceland furnished fertile land and enough sources for the Viking settlers. The colonization of Iceland turn out to be driven by using using the use of a choice to break out political turmoil, installation new organizations, and searching for greater autonomy. The sagas, literary narratives that mix facts and fable, recount the disturbing situations and triumphs of these early settlers, painting a glittery photograph of the hardships they confronted and the resilience that defined their endeavors.

Greenland have end up some other huge tour spot for Viking exploration. In the early tenth century, Erik the Red set up a colony on Greenland's western coast. The call "Greenland" itself became likely a strategic preference, designed to draw settlers to a land that skilled harsh winters. The Greenland colony thrived for severa centuries, with the Vikings adapting to the surroundings and subsisting via farming, searching, and trade. The Vinland sagas, part of Norse literature, propose that Viking explorers may furthermore have ventured as some distance as North America, likely attaining current-day-day Newfoundland in Canada.

The Vikings' effect extended to the British Isles and Ireland, in which they set up settlements and trading posts. The Danelaw, a region in England, modified into characterised thru Viking affect on language, governance, and culture. The Viking presence furthermore left an indelible mark on the Irish landscape, as Viking warriors, investors, and settlers interacted with close by corporations, contributing to a fusion of cultural factors that keeps to resonate in cutting-edge-day Ireland.

The Varangian Guard, an elite unit of Viking warriors, ventured eastward to function mercenaries inside the Byzantine Empire. These skilled opponents earned the honor of Byzantine emperors and played a massive function in Byzantine politics and military campaigns. Their presence in Constantinople, the capital of the Byzantine Empire, added about cultural exchanges and interactions that enriched every societies.

The Viking voyages of exploration were fueled with the aid of a multifaceted combination of motivations. Economic aspirations, collectively with the search for valuable sources and change possibilities, drove masses of these trips. The choice for popularity and glory additionally finished a vital position, as a success expeditions have been celebrated and extended the reputation of explorers within their agencies. Additionally, the Vikings' thirst for adventure and hobby approximately the arena round them have been critical to their willingness to undertake perilous trips into the unknown.

In forestall, the exploration of recent lands throughout the Viking Age represents a remarkable financial disaster in human statistics. The Vikings' navigational prowess, maritime innovation, and resilience enabled them to traverse huge distances, encountering numerous cultures and shaping the destinies of regions an prolonged manner from their homelands. These voyages of exploration now not most effective extended geographical know-how however additionally facilitated cultural exchanges that enriched the tapestry of human revel in. The legacy of Viking exploration endures as a testomony to the indomitable spirit of human hobby and the iconic impact of these intrepid adventurers at the direction of facts.

Chapter 3: Viking Age Monarchs And Leaders

The Viking Age modified into characterized through a dynamic political panorama, shaped by using the usage of using the management of monarchs, chieftains, and leaders who accomplished pivotal roles inside the governance, increase, and cultural evolution of Viking societies. These figures wielded impact through a combination of navy prowess, diplomacy, and the capability to consistent the loyalty and appreciate of their enthusiasts, leaving an indelible mark on the information of the generation.

Viking societies had been organized into clans, tribes, and chiefdoms, every led thru a chieftain or close by leader. These leaders were chargeable for maintaining social order, resolving disputes, and presenting protection to their communities. As areas extended and interactions with neighboring societies extended, the jobs and electricity dynamics of these leaders superior, giving rise to more complicated political systems.

In addition to close by leaders, the Viking Age observed the emergence of monarchs who held authority over larger territories. Legendary figures collectively with Harald Fairhair of Norway and Gorm the Old of Denmark are awesome examples of Viking monarchs who sought to consolidate energy and extend their geographical regions. Harald Fairhair's unification of Norway marked a large milestone, as he labored to set up a centralized monarchy and impose his rule over previously disparate areas.

Leadership in Viking societies grow to be frequently intertwined with martial prowess. The capability to manual warriors into struggle and advantage victories on the field of fight become a defining function of a successful leader. Battles and conquests had been instrumental in improving a pacesetter's popularity and standing, earning them the loyalty of their lovers. The sagas often celebrated leaders who examined terrific bravery, cunning, and tactical acumen in battle.

While struggle became a great issue of control, diplomatic skills had been furthermore essential. Alliances, treaties, and negotiations done a important function in keeping balance and securing assets. The leaders who excelled at global individuals of the family often determined themselves in fantastic positions, capable of leverage relationships with neighboring societies for mutual gain.

The complicated net of management in Viking societies grow to be no longer restricted to men. Women additionally held positions of effect, especially within the context of familial and familial roles.

Some girls, regularly known as "shieldmaidens," were famend for his or her fight competencies and management abilties. Additionally, queens and noblewomen wielded authority and impact in topics of governance, worldwide family members, and cultural affairs.

The concept of a Thing, an assembly in which freemen gathered to make picks and remedy disputes, changed into valuable to Viking political life. These gatherings allowed leaders to talk with their topics, talk subjects of significance, and make picks that impacted the community. The Thing exemplified the participatory nature of Viking governance, wherein leaders needed to earn the recall and beneficial useful resource in their human beings thru their moves and choices.

As the Viking Age advanced, the political landscape persisted to adapt. The impact of monarchs stepped forward, and territories have been divided into smaller administrative devices governed by way of jarls, nearby rulers appointed with the beneficial aid of the monarchs. The unfold of Christianity furthermore added adjustments to management structures, as church officers acquired effect along secular leaders.

In very last, Viking Age monarchs and leaders had been pivotal figures who fashioned the future of their societies and left an extended lasting effect on statistics. Their manage patterns, whether or not or no longer characterized with the useful useful resource of army prowess, diplomatic finesse, or a aggregate of each, contemplated the complexity of Viking societies and their interactions with the broader international. The roles of chieftains, monarchs, and one in all a kind leaders contributed to the dynamic tapestry of Viking subculture, governance, and the evolution of political systems that preserve to intrigue and encourage to nowadays.

The Art of War: Weapons and Tactics

In the Viking Age, the artwork of warfare emerge as a defining factor of the way of existence, shaping each the society's shielding talents and its ability for conquest. The Vikings' functionality in warfare have become manifested through a mixture of present day weaponry, strategic techniques, and a warrior ethos that permeated every aspect in their lifestyles.

At the coronary coronary heart of Viking conflict have been numerous guns, every tailored to specific combat conditions. The sword, a photo of repute and electricity, have emerge as a crucial weapon within the arsenal of Viking warriors. These swords, often characterised through their double-edged blades and complex hilts, were now not most effective beneficial but moreover ornamental, reflecting the warrior's recognition and prowess.

Axes, both unmarried- and double-bladed, were any other signature weapon of the Vikings. These bendy weapons were used for pretty quite a number fight conditions, from close-quarters combat to throwing in warfare. The overall performance and brutality of Viking awl assaults have been more appropriate through manner of the brutal strain and momentum generated via their wielders.

Spears, with their obtain and piercing capability, were essential to Viking methods. The spear modified into not only a weapon of offense however moreover an device of safety, allowing warriors to preserve their adversaries at bay. Skilled spearmen have to use those guns to create an exceptional barrier in the direction of charging fighters, exploiting their acquire to manipulate the battlefield.

Bows and arrows have been utilized for ranged combat, permitting the Vikings to have interaction enemies from a distance. Archery have turn out to be a valued expertise, specifically for raiders and warriors conducting hit-and-run strategies. The use of bows allowed the Vikings to weaken their foes earlier than carrying out close to combat, presenting a strategic gain that changed into further amplified with the aid in their skills in marksmanship.

Shields were an critical problem of Viking struggle, serving as both safety and tactical system. Shields numerous in size and design, with a few designed for man or woman protection and others supposed for forming protect walls. The latter allowed Viking warriors to create an excellent barrier toward enemy attacks, making it hard for adversaries to breach their defenses.

The Vikings' tactical facts extended past person weaponry to encompass strategic maneuvers and formations. The protect wall, a defensive formation in which warriors stood aspect with the useful resource of way of aspect, interlocking their shields to create an impregnable barrier, changed right into a signature tactic of Viking conflict. This formation maximized the collective strength of the squaddies, turning the tide of battle in their pick.

Raiding modified proper right into a cornerstone of Viking war, characterised thru wonder assaults on coastal settlements and monasteries. The longships' shallow drafts allowed the Vikings to navigate rivers and approach their goals with stealth. Once on land, the raiders might hire hit-and-run techniques, leveraging their pace and understanding of the terrain to strike abruptly and retreat earlier than reinforcements need to arrive.

The psychology of worry and intimidation come to be an vital factor of Viking battle. The look of Viking warriors, with their precise helmets, armor, and fierce countenances, struck terror into the hearts of their foes. The berserkers, legendary warriors who entered conflict in a frenzy-like nation, in addition amplified the mental effect, making the Vikings' recognition as fearsome warriors a powerful weapon in itself.

In end, the art of warfare within the Viking Age modified right into a multi-faceted location that encompassed weapons, techniques, and a totally precise warrior ethos. The Vikings' weaponry, characterised by the use of swords, axes, spears, and bows, showcased their innovation and flexibility in combat eventualities. Their strategic prowess, at the side of guard walls and raiding techniques, displayed their capability to interact in every organized battles and hit-and-run raids. The mental factors of battle, from the intimidating appearance of Viking warriors to the ferocity of the berserkers, added a psychological length to their martial approach. The legacy of the Viking technique to war endures as a testomony to their resourcefulness, courage, and the profound impact their art of struggle left on statistics.

Women in Viking Society

In the difficult tapestry of Viking society, women occupied roles that have been numerous, multifaceted, and vital to the functioning in their agencies. While the triumphing photograph of Vikings often emphasizes the male warrior archetype, the reality became a complicated blend of gender roles that encompassed the whole lot from domestic duties to participation in trade, governance, or perhaps struggle.

Viking ladies's roles have been inspired thru using a variety of factors, which includes social fame, vicinity, and individual times. At the coronary coronary heart of Viking households, ladies finished vast roles in coping with domestic affairs, which encompassed duties along with cooking, cloth production, and baby-rearing. Their obligations extended past mere homemaking; women were critical to the economic balance in their families and, with the aid of way of extension, their companies.

Agriculture modified right into a cornerstone of Viking life, and girls played critical roles in tending to vegetation, worrying for livestock, and keeping meals through strategies like salting, drying, and fermenting. The domestic competencies of women were instrumental in making sure the survival and prosperity of their households, underpinning the Viking manner of lifestyles.

Despite the regularly prevailing patriarchal structures, ladies in Viking society held positions of authority and feature an effect on. Noblewomen, frequently known as "gyðjas" or "seeresses," held spiritual and ceremonial roles, serving as priestesses and oracles. These ladies had the energy to speak with the divine and provide steering to their groups, showcasing the honor accorded to their insights.

Trade and alternate were domains wherein Viking girls completed vital roles. Women were lively participants in community markets, regularly attractive within the shopping for and selling of merchandise. Additionally, archaeological proof shows that women can also were involved in prolonged-distance change, accompanying their male opposite numbers on trips and contributing to the exchange of precious assets and cultural influences.

The sagas, historic narratives that blend fact and delusion, offer glimpses into the lives of outstanding Viking girls. Figures like Lagertha and Freydis Eiriksdottir are celebrated for their feats in combat and their roles in shaping Viking data. These sagas, at the same time as from time to time embellished with mythical factors, highlight the life of women who defied societal norms and completed renown in domain names traditionally related to men.

Viking girls's agency prolonged to subjects of governance and desire-making. In the absence of male leaders because of battle or remarkable events, girls ought to anticipate leadership roles, wielding strength and authority over their groups. Additionally, girls played diplomatic roles, negotiating marriages and alliances that contributed to the political balance of Viking society.

Viking Age burial internet websites provide belief into the social fame of ladies. Some women were buried with precious artifacts, emphasizing their reputation and roles inside their communities. These burials show off that women's contributions to society were stated and respected, even in a patriarchal context.

The concept of "fosterage" end up a shape of social bonding in Viking society. Children, collectively with the ones of the Aristocracy, have been regularly despatched to be fostered via distinctive families. This exercising allowed ladies to persuade the upbringing of younger individuals, presenting cultural values, abilities, and know-how.

In the sector of conflict, whilst Viking girls did now not generally engage in warfare as warriors, they were now not definitely excluded from navy contexts. Women held the responsibility of defensive their houses and communities in instances of war. Archaeological findings advise that some girls had been buried with guns, likely indicating a symbolic or practical connection to protection.

In cease, girls in Viking society occupied a spectrum of roles that extended an prolonged way beyond the conventional dichotomy of the house sphere in area of the battlefield. Their contributions to economics, governance, religion, and cultural trade have been instrumental in shaping the cloth of Viking groups. While societal norms diverse, Viking girls's agency, resilience, and multifaceted contributions have left an indelible mark on statistics, providing a more nuanced and dynamic angle at the position of girls in societies of the past.

Chapter 4: Trade And Economic Networks

In the complex internet of Viking society, exchange and exchange had been threads that wove through the fabric of each day life, connecting remote lands and cultures in a network of financial change. The Vikings' prowess as seafarers and their strategic geographic role allowed them to forge extensive alternate routes, enriching their societies and facilitating cultural interactions that left an extended-lasting impact on statistics.

Central to the Viking Age's economic networks have been the enduring longships, vessels that now not fantastic enabled raids and exploration however furthermore facilitated trade throughout super distances. These versatile ships allowed the Vikings to navigate rivers, seas, and oceans, accomplishing places that have been previously inaccessible. The longships' shallow drafts enabled them to journey along rivers and installation alternate connections with inland companies, developing a multifaceted community that spanned from Scandinavia to Constantinople and past.

One of the Viking Age's awesome exchange routes modified into the "Silver Road," a maritime exchange route that related Scandinavia to the Byzantine Empire. This path facilitated the change of treasured commodities, which incorporates furs, wood, and slaves from the North for silver, spices, and luxury objects from the East. The wealth generated from this trade strengthened the economies of every Viking territories and Byzantine cities.

Another key trade direction end up the "Amber Road," which facilitated the movement of amber from the Baltic area to markets inside the Mediterranean.

Amber, prized for its beauty and perceived magical houses, become in excessive name for amongst numerous cultures. Viking traders done a critical position in the distribution of amber, further improving their economic have an impact on and cultural connections.

Viking change extended past physical gadgets to embody cultural exchange, because of the fact the interactions with distant places lands introduced new ideas, technology, and imaginative influences. The Vikings' encounters with cultures as various as the ones of the Middle East, Ireland, and Russia brought about the fusion of ingenious styles, the advent of foreign craftsmanship strategies, and the spread of improvements consisting of coin minting.

The repute quo of buying and selling posts and settlements alongside trade routes reinforced monetary sports and interactions. The buying and selling city of Birka in Sweden, as an example, served as a hub for shoppers and artisans, in which devices from near and a ways were exchanged. The metropolis's archaeological stays offer insights into the bustling financial lifestyles of the Viking Age, showcasing the wide style of items that circulated thru those networks.

In addition to worldwide trade, Viking society furthermore featured neighborhood and nearby markets that facilitated the exchange of products and assets. These markets, regularly held at crossroads or close to large settlements, allowed for the alternate of merchandise collectively with textiles, foodstuffs, and metalwork. The economy's vibrancy changed into similarly supported through way of know-how, with skilled artisans producing gadgets of utilitarian and ornamental rate.

The Vikings' impact on the territories they visited extended past trade, as they often installation relationships with close by rulers and communities. These alliances may want to bring about together beneficial arrangements, including exchange privileges and steady passage. The Vikings' recognition as professional warriors and seafarers moreover contributed to their have an impact on in negotiations and exchange agreements.

In last, exchange and monetary networks were essential to the vibrancy and complexity of Viking society. The interconnectedness facilitated through the Vikings' maritime talents and buying and promoting networks created a dynamic economic panorama that enriched their cultures, enabled cultural change, and induced the development of regions a protracted manner past their homelands. The legacy of the Vikings' economic endeavors stays felt inside the shared cultural ancient past and international connections which have continued via the passage of time.

Runes and Writing System

In the charming realm of Viking tradition, runes held a unique and profound importance as each a writing tool and a form of cultural expression. The runic alphabet, referred to as the "Futhark," consisted of a difficult and speedy of characters that have been no longer without a doubt symbols for verbal exchange but also carried non secular and magical connotations. The runes have been more than a way of conveying information; they were a conduit for the sacred, a mirrored image of the Viking worldview, and a key element of their identity.

The runic alphabet, in the starting which includes 24 characters, developed through the years and became used for numerous functions. The runes had been now not only hired for writing inscriptions on gadgets however moreover for casting divinations and invoking magic. This multifaceted nature of runes highlights their primary feature in Viking spirituality, wherein the written phrase modified into seen as a strong device for talking with the divine and influencing the natural global.

Runestones, huge stones adorned with runic inscriptions, have been prominent functions of Viking landscapes. These stones served as markers for graves, memorials, and expressions of reputation. The inscriptions on runestones commemorated people, their achievements, and their connections to the geographical regions of the residing and the vain. Each runestone's inscription supplied a window into the social, familial, and personal components of Viking lifestyles.

The makes use of of runes extended beyond the physical realm. Seeresses and diviners hired runes for casting hundreds and foretelling the future. The act of casting runes, called "casting the runes" or "throwing the runes," become a form of verbal exchange with the spirit international, providing steering, omens, and insights into the unknown. This exercising showcased the belief that the runes possessed an innate electricity to reveal hidden truths and faucet into the paranormal.

Runes additionally performed a position in Viking craftsmanship, acting on numerous artifacts starting from guns and jewelry to system and regular gadgets. These inscriptions imbued gadgets with magical protection, honoring deities, or serving as markers of ownership. The exercise of inscribing runes on devices combined the practical with the mystical, reflecting the interwoven nature of spirituality and the cloth worldwide in Viking culture.

The runic alphabet changed into divided into superb units or "futharks," each comprising a totally specific affiliation of characters. The Elder Futhark, the earliest regarded form of the runic alphabet, contained 24 characters. Over time, this superior into the Younger Futhark, which consisted of sixteen characters. The runic characters themselves were angular and smooth, making them suitable for carving into wood, stone, and metallic.

While runes were critical to Viking subculture, their usage declined with the unfold of Christianity and the adoption of the Latin alphabet for writing. As Christian impacts obtained prominence, the association of runes with pagan ideals brought about their dwindled use for inscriptions. However, the legacy of runes endured thru the upkeep of runic inscriptions on stones, artifacts, and manuscripts, imparting cutting-edge college students with worthwhile insights into Viking information, language, and beliefs.

In end, runes and the runic writing device held a multifaceted position in Viking tradition. They had been symbols of communique, magic, spirituality, and identity, supplying a window into the worldview and practices of the Vikings. The legacy of runes keeps to fascinate and captivate contemporary audiences, serving as a bridge that connects us to the wealthy tapestry of the Viking Age and the complex interplay a few of the mundane and the magical in their society.

The Danelaw: Viking Influence in England

The Viking Age witnessed the emergence of the Danelaw, a very specific and fascinating economic catastrophe in the records of England that showcased the Vikings' effect on governance, regulation, culture, and society. The term "Danelaw" said the place of England in which Danish Vikings established a full-size presence, leaving an indelible mark at the panorama, establishments, and cultural cloth of the land.

The origins of the Danelaw can be traced another time to the overdue ninth century, at the same time as Viking raiders and settlers started to exert have an effect on over elements of England. The time period "Danelaw" itself is concept to were derived from the Old Norse words "dane" (Danes) and "lag" (law), indicating the imposition of Danish criminal and administrative structures in the territories they controlled.

The Danelaw encompassed a full-size part of japanese and northerly England, which incorporates regions which include Northumbria, East Anglia, and additives of Mercia. In those areas, Viking impact changed into felt not only in terms of governance however additionally via linguistic, cultural, and economic interactions. Viking settlers set up businesses, intermingling with the nearby Anglo-Saxon population and contributing to a fusion of traditions.

One of the most sizable elements of the Danelaw have turn out to be its prison device. The Vikings introduced their personal jail codes, referred to as "Danelaw codes," which have been amazing from the Anglo-Saxon jail traditions of the time. These codes, which incorporates the "Gulaþingslög" in the Danelaw of York, represented a blend of Viking and Anglo-Saxon affects and pondered the complex interactions some of the 2 cultures. The prison framework of the Danelaw examined the Vikings' capacity to evolve and coexist with the close by populace even as keeping their notable identity.

Trade and trade thrived within the Danelaw, contributing to economic boom and cultural exchange. The Vikings' expertise in seafaring and change routes facilitated the glide of merchandise and thoughts amongst England, Scandinavia, and one of a kind elements of Europe. The Danelaw's strategic vicinity alongside navigable rivers and coastlines greater its repute as a hub for change, and this monetary pastime left an prolonged-lasting imprint on the area's improvement.

Language and linguistic have an effect on had been vital to the Danelaw's legacy. While Old English remained the dominant language, the Vikings' linguistic contributions were obvious in place names, private names, and linguistic loanwords. These linguistic remnants pondered the interactions amongst Viking settlers and the prevailing population, underscoring the complicated cultural exchange that described the Danelaw.

Religious interactions were each other side of Viking effect in the Danelaw. The Vikings' religious practices and beliefs, often rooted in Norse mythology, coexisted alongside Christianity. In some times, pagan practices and Christian traditions intertwined, giving rise to a syncretic shape of spirituality. The interplay among the ones religious structures presented a completely unique glimpse into the complexities of religion finally of this transformative duration.

The Danelaw's importance prolonged beyond its proper now technology, because it left an indelible mark on the historical trajectory of England. The Viking presence and feature an impact on in the Danelaw contributed to the broader narrative of English information, shaping cultural dynamics, jail frameworks, and the intercultural change that described the location.

In conclusion, the Danelaw represents a pivotal financial disaster within the Viking Age and English history. The Vikings' established order of governance, felony structures, monetary networks, and cultural interactions in the Danelaw showcased their adaptability, their capacity to coexist with gift populations, and their capability to leave an prolonged-lasting legacy on the territories they advocated. The Danelaw's complicated interplay of cultures, traditions, and institutions maintains to intrigue students and enthusiasts alike, offering a window into the dynamic nature of Viking engagement with the broader international.

Chapter 5: Skalds And Norse Poetry

In the difficult tapestry of Viking way of life, the art work of poetry held unique vicinity as a form of cultural expression, entertainment, and historical documentation. Skalds, the professional poets of Norse society, have been reputable for his or her functionality to craft tough verses that conveyed not handiest narratives and sagas but additionally the very essence of Viking worldviews, ideals, and heroic beliefs.

Skaldic poetry changed into characterized via its complicated and problematic form. Skalds employed tricky meters, kennings (metaphorical descriptions), and alliterations to create verses that were every melodious and significant. The skaldic artistry often extended past the written phrase, as poets might carry out their compositions orally, mission contests of wit and poetic potential called "flyting."

The sagas, ancient narratives that blend facts and fable, frequently factor out skalds and their contributions to Viking society. These poets served as oral historians, preserving the testimonies of mythical figures, heroic feats, and large events. The artwork of skaldic poetry modified into a vital approach of passing down cultural records and preserving the collective memory of the Viking Age.

Skalds had the capacity to immortalize human beings and their deeds through poetry. Kings, warriors, and leaders sought to advantage the select of skalds, as their verses need to solidify their legacy for generations to go back. The sagas are replete with times of skalds composing "drápur" (praise poems) and "kviðuháttr" (warrior verses) that celebrated the achievements and valor of terrific figures.

The skaldic way of life changed into carefully associated with Norse mythology and cosmology. Poems frequently protected references to gods, goddesses, and mythical creatures, bridging the space some of the mortal and divine geographical regions. Skalds' capacity to weave mythological factors into their compositions brought a layer of depth and resonance, connecting the human experience to the cosmic order.

Eddic poetry, some distinctive shape of Norse poetry, existed in tandem with skaldic poetry. Eddic poems, gathered inside the "Edda" texts, have been characterized thru their starkness and narrative cognizance. These poems stated reminiscences from Norse mythology, presenting insights into the gods, advent myths, and the cataclysmic events of Ragnarök.

The feature of skalds prolonged beyond leisure; additionally they accomplished diplomatic and political features. Skaldic poetry modified into used in courts as a technique of praising rulers, forging alliances, and solidifying political relationships. The poems served as a form of international relations, with poets composing verses that flattered and commemorated their clients at the same time as conveying messages to the broader worldwide.

Skaldic poetry underwent intervals of evolution, inspired with the resource of way of converting social and cultural dynamics. The shift from pagan traditions to the unfold of Christianity delivered changes to the skaldic paintings shape. Some skalds incorporated Christian problem subjects and imagery into their poetry, reflecting the affect of the state-of-the-art religion on cultural expressions.

The legacy of skaldic poetry endures to in recent times through the written records which have survived. The Edda texts and other belongings offer modern-day scholars with insights into the complicated linguistic systems, metaphors, and concern subjects of skaldic poetry. The cultural impact of skalds' artwork stays obtrusive in current-day appreciation for the sagas, myths, and narratives that the ones poets preserved and celebrated.

In conclusion, skalds and Norse poetry normal an vital a part of Viking way of life, supplying a window into the hearts, minds, and ideals of the people of the time. Skaldic artistry modified right into a repository of history, myth, and identity, bridging the space a few of the mundane and the paranormal, the spoken and the written. The legacy of skalds lives on as a testomony to the long-lasting energy of poetry to seize the essence of an technology and to carry the depth and complexity of the human enjoy.

Settlements and Urban Life

In the colourful tapestry of Viking society, settlements and concrete facilities emerged as pivotal hubs of monetary interest, cultural change, and governance. While the well-known picture of the Vikings frequently makes a speciality of their maritime exploits, the fact turn out to be a dynamic community of settlements that ranged from small farming organizations to bustling buying and selling towns, each contributing to the richness and complexity of Viking lifestyles.

The Vikings hooked up a severa variety of settlements at some stage in their territories, reflecting the severa landscapes and natural assets to be had. These settlements were positioned alongside rivers, coastlines, and fertile valleys, considering clean get right of entry to to transportation, exchange routes, and agricultural land. As a surrender end result, settlements flourished as centers of agriculture, trade, and craftsmanship.

Urban facilities, characterized with the useful resource of fortified walls, marketplaces, and administrative buildings, served as hubs of activity and cultural exchange. These cities were frequently strategically placed alongside change routes and coastal regions, permitting the Vikings to engage in prolonged-distance exchange and set up connections with neighboring areas. Urban life supplied a evaluation to the rural lifestyle, providing possibilities for social interactions, trade, and cultural mingling.

Trading cities, which include Birka in Sweden and Hedeby in Denmark, exemplified the financial vibrancy of city Viking settlements. These towns had been bustling with traders, artisans, and visitors from near and a ways. The presence of an prepared marketplace facilitated the exchange of merchandise starting from meals and textiles to highly-priced devices and extraordinary imports. The fulfillment of these shopping for and selling towns have become carefully tied to their strategic places and the community of connections they facilitated.

Craftsmanship performed a pivotal feature in the financial and cultural existence of Viking settlements. Skilled artisans produced a massive form of products, which includes rings, textiles, weapons, and gear. The great of workmanship in Viking settlements become famend, and their wares have been modern through using each community groups and far flung searching for and selling companions. The artisans' creations not most effective furnished practical application but moreover served as expressions of cultural identification and standing.

Agriculture regular the backbone of Viking settlements, retaining community populations and allowing the growth of town facilities. The fertile lands surrounding settlements had been cultivated for vegetation together with barley, rye, oats, and wheat. Livestock rearing, which include farm animals, sheep, and pigs, supplemented the meals deliver and furnished uncooked substances for textiles and leather-based totally-primarily based goods. The interaction among agricultural production and urban intake long-established a symbiotic dating that fueled the growth of Viking society.

The political and administrative factors of Viking settlements severa primarily based on factors which consist of vicinity, length, and nearby control. Some settlements have been governed via way of chieftains or community leaders who oversaw topics of justice, dispute selection, and useful aid allocation. Larger city centers often had more complex administrative structures, with appointed officials and felony suggestions that regulated exchange, assets rights, and social interactions.

Religion and spirituality were woven into the cloth of urban existence. Settlements often had primary collecting places for communal rituals and ceremonies. Temples, regularly devoted to gods and goddesses together with Odin, Thor, and Freyja, have been critical to the spiritual lifestyles of the network. These places of worship were venues for offerings, sacrifices, and gatherings that strengthened the relationship the various mortal realm and the divine.

As city facilities flourished, interactions with neighboring cultures have turn out to be extra normal. The Vikings' encounters with precise cultures via exchange, worldwide family members, and conquest facilitated the exchange of mind, technologies, and innovative impacts. These interactions enriched the cultural tapestry of Viking society, shaping city existence and contributing to the cosmopolitan surroundings of settlements.

In closing, settlements and concrete existence have been essential additives of Viking society, fostering economic, cultural, and social dynamism. From small farming groups to bustling shopping for and selling towns, those settlements performed a crucial function in shaping the Viking Age. The vibrancy of urban facilities, the change of products and mind, and the interactions with neighboring cultures all contributed to the complicated and multifaceted nature of Viking society, leaving an indelible mark on data and provoking persevered fascination and exploration.

The Varangian Guard: Vikings in Byzantium

In the annals of statistics, the Vikings' effect extended a long way past their homelands, attaining the remote seashores of the Byzantine Empire. The Varangian Guard, a mythical pressure of Viking warriors, served as a testament to the Vikings' prowess as mercenaries, their capability to comply to overseas cultures, and their effect on the world degree.

The Varangian Guard, called "Varangians," have been a tremendous presence in the Byzantine Empire from the tenth to the 14th centuries. These Viking warriors, drawn from the Scandinavian homelands and one among a type components of Europe, became an crucial part of the Byzantine army and the elite corps of the Emperor's personal bodyguard. The Varangians' reputation for bravery, loyalty, and combat know-how made them exceptionally stylish with the aid of way of the Byzantine rulers.

The Varangian Guard's origins may be traced once more to the early tenth century even as the Byzantine Empire began out to recruit Scandinavian warriors as a part of their popularity military. The Varangians introduced with them their special fighting styles, weaponry, and warrior ethos, developing a totally specific aggregate of Viking and Byzantine army traditions. This fusion of cultures resulted in an outstanding stress that mixed the Vikings' fierce fight talents with Byzantine tactical sophistication.

The Varangian Guard's feature extended beyond army duties. They have been regularly employed in ceremonial abilties, serving as honor guards at some point of imperial processions and ceremonies. The Varangians' presence added an air of prestige and mystique to the Byzantine court docket, showcasing the Emperor's functionality to command a stress of top notch and famend warriors.

The Varangian Guard's loyalty changed into a prized trait. They were seemed for his or her steadfast allegiance to the Byzantine Emperor, often forming private bonds with the rulers they served. This loyalty was reflected in their protection of the Emperor, even within the face of overwhelming odds. The Varangians' self-control to their oath of protection earned them the remember and recognize of the Byzantine elite.

The Varangian Guard additionally played a vital characteristic in pivotal moments of Byzantine information. Their participation in battles consisting of the Battle of Dyrrhachium and the Battle of Manzikert showcased their martial prowess and their effect at the consequences of historic conflicts. The Varangians' functionality to reveal the tide of battle and function elite surprise troops became instrumental in shaping the route of Byzantine military campaigns.

Despite their overseas origins, the Varangians regularly assimilated into Byzantine society. Over time, they married Byzantine girls, discovered the Greek language, and observed factors of Byzantine way of life. This cultural exchange enriched each the Varangians and the Byzantines, contributing to the cosmopolitan environment of the Byzantine Empire.

The Varangian Guard's have an effect on prolonged beyond the army sphere. They contributed to Byzantine innovative and cultural history thru their interactions with neighborhood populations. The Varangians' presence in Constantinople, the Byzantine capital, left a tangible mark at the town's architectural panorama, influencing the improvement of church homes, fortifications, and unique structures.

The decline of the Varangian Guard reflected the broader shifts in Byzantine statistics. As the Byzantine Empire confronted inner strife, outside threats, and changing army strategies, the Varangians' position underwent adjustments. While their numbers diminished over time, their legacy persevered in the collective memory of the Byzantine Empire and the annals of statistics.

In conclusion, the Varangian Guard represented the Vikings' amazing capability to comply, assimilate, and make their mark on foreign lands. Their presence within the Byzantine Empire showcased the Vikings' reputation as fierce warriors, their capability to feature cultural ambassadors, and their effect at the dynamics of a long way-accomplishing empires. The Varangian Guard's story is a testament to the iconic legacy of the Vikings, whose have an impact on reached past their homelands to form the narratives of civilizations across the world.

Chapter 6: Maritime Heritage And Ship Burials

In the complicated weave of Viking way of lifestyles, the sea comes to be each a lifeline and a gateway to exploration, trade, and conquest. The Vikings' mastery of maritime abilities and their deep connection to the waters that surrounded their homelands left a long lasting legacy that shaped their society, beliefs, and burial practices.

The maritime background of the Vikings comes to be rooted in their intimate relationship with the sea. The geographical format of Scandinavia, with its elaborate network of fjords, rivers, and coastal areas, facilitated the Vikings' development of superior shipbuilding strategies. The iconic Viking longships, characterised by way in their easy design and shallow drafts, have been versatile vessels that allowed the Vikings to navigate every open seas and inland waterways effortlessly.

These longships, often organized with every sails and oars, enabled the Vikings to embark on some distance-undertaking expeditions. From raiding the coasts of England and France to setting up change routes with distant lands, the Vikings' maritime capabilities spread out possibilities for exploration, commerce, and cultural change. The format in their ships not great facilitated the ones sports activities however additionally became symbols of the Vikings' prowess and identification.

The significance of ships prolonged past the region of the residing. Ship burials, a workout precise to Viking way of existence, have been a testament to the Vikings' beliefs approximately the afterlife and their connection to the ocean. Ship burials involved placing the deceased, together with their belongings and regularly sacrificed animals, on a in particular built supply. This supply end up then set ablaze or buried as part of a funerary ritual that commemorated the character's life and ensured their stable passage to the world of the vain.

The maximum famous example of a supply burial is the Oseberg Ship Burial, determined in Norway. The Oseberg burial, courting decrease lower back to the 9th century, contained the remains of two girls and a wealth of artifacts, dropping moderate on Viking society, craftsmanship, and burial practices. The supply itself modified into ornately adorned, showcasing the complicated carvings and innovative competencies of the time.

Ship burials had been now not constrained to the Scandinavian homelands. The Vikings' maritime have an effect on prolonged to areas they encountered at some point of their voyages. In regions along with the British Isles and Russia, supply burials have been determined, suggesting that the Vikings' belief in the connection amongst ships and the afterlife transcended geographical boundaries.

The practice of ship burials presentations the Vikings' worldview, in which the ocean held spiritual significance and modified proper into a conduit between the geographical areas of the living and the useless. The deliver itself represented a vessel for the soul's journey to the afterlife, reflecting the Vikings' perception inside the cyclical nature of lifestyles and lack of life. The inclusion of grave objects and sacrificed animals established the Vikings' desire to provide for the deceased within the afterlife.

Ship burials have been part of a larger complicated of burial practices in Viking society. Alongside deliver burials, specific varieties of burial, collectively with mound burials and cremations, showcased the form of ideals and cultural expressions indoors Viking organizations. Ship burials, but, stood out as amazing and iconic representations of the Vikings' maritime ancient past and their connection to the natural global.

The legacy of the Vikings' maritime records and deliver burials endures in current instances. Archaeological discoveries, at the side of the Gokstad and Oseberg ships, preserve to offer insights into Viking shipbuilding techniques, craftsmanship, and funerary practices. Museums and exhibitions round the world show off those artifacts, permitting current audiences to glimpse the majesty of Viking ships and the cultural significance of supply burials.

In remaining, the maritime records of the Vikings and their exercising of ship burials form a charming financial smash in the tapestry of Viking way of life. The sea, with its realistic and non secular significance, emerge as a using pressure that usual the Vikings' way of life. Ship burials, as a very precise and evocative burial exercise, characteristic a testomony to the Vikings' ideals, their connection to the sea, and their choice to honor and keep the recollections of their departed. The legacy of Viking maritime traditions keeps to inspire awe and hobby, offering a glimpse into the elaborate layers of Viking identity and the enduring effect in their seafaring legacy.

Viking Age Art and Craftsmanship

Within the hard tapestry of Viking lifestyle, artwork and craftsmanship emerged as vibrant expressions of the society's ideals, values, and aesthetic sensibilities. From intricately designed jewelry to elegantly carved timber artifacts, the Vikings' artistic creations showcased their creativity, talent, and cultural identification.

Viking Age art became deeply intertwined with each day lifestyles and pondered the interplay of practicality and splendor. Craftsmen, along with blacksmiths, jewelers, weavers, and woodcarvers, honed their skills to create gadgets that have been now not pleasant useful but additionally decorated with complicated designs and symbolism. The Vikings' mastery of numerous materials, in conjunction with steel, bone, timber, and textiles, allowed them to craft gadgets of each realistic use and aesthetic attraction.

Jewelry emerge as a prominent issue of Viking artistry, regularly worn as reputation symbols, amulets, and expressions of identity. Brooches, necklaces, and rings have been intricately designed, with motifs starting from complex knots to animal paperwork. The use of precious metals along side gold and silver showcased the Vikings' access to valuable assets and their appreciation for craftsmanship.

Metalwork held a completely unique area in Viking artwork, with professional blacksmiths generating a big range of devices, at the side of guns, tool, and ornamental devices. Swords, axes, and spears were now not most effective devices of struggle but moreover canvases for problematic engravings and ornamentation. The hard styles and designs on those guns contemplated the Vikings' belief in imbuing items with non secular and shielding inclinations.

Woodcarving became a few other sizable element of Viking craftsmanship, with artisans developing problematic styles and motifs on wooden gadgets in conjunction with longships, sledges, and everyday tools. The Oseberg Ship's ornate carvings, depicting intertwining animals and complex shapes, exemplify the meticulous hobby to detail that characterised Viking woodwork.

Textile manufacturing become an essential talent that contributed to the Vikings' cloth life-style and self-sufficiency. The Vikings had been adept at weaving textiles from wool and flax, growing cloth for apparel, sails, and domestic use. The problematic styles and designs on woven cloth not first-rate proven technical understanding however moreover served as a way of personal expression.

Artistic motifs frequently protected elements from Norse mythology, animals, and geometric patterns. Animals which includes wolves, ravens, and serpents were routine motifs in Viking paintings, regularly symbolizing one-of-a-kind additives of the herbal worldwide and mythology. Geometric patterns, consisting of the "Valknut" (knot of the slain warriors), held symbolic importance and represented the interconnectedness of lifestyles and loss of life.

Viking artwork become not restricted to character objects; it prolonged to massive architectural and sculptural paperwork. Runestones, erected as memorials and markers, featured carvings of every human figures and mythological scenes. The Gotland Picture Stones, as an example, depicted scenes from Norse myths, battles, and every day life, offering a visible narrative that enriched our know-how of Viking lifestyle.

The Vikings' creative expressions additionally reached beyond their homelands thru their vast change networks. Viking buyers and raiders added domestic treasures and inventive impacts from remote lands, contributing to the cultural change and enrichment in their society. This trade is apparent in artifacts that feature foreign places progressive motifs and techniques, reflecting the Vikings' open-mindedness to new mind and forms.

Viking art and craftsmanship held cultural and social significance, reflecting no longer remarkable revolutionary capability but moreover the values and aspirations of the society. Objects created through those abilities often served as markers of reputation, non-public identity, and connections to the supernatural. The exercise of imparting valuable gadgets in burials underscored the importance of these artifacts within the afterlife.

In present day-day times, Viking art work continues to captivate cutting-edge audiences via museum exhibitions, instructional studies, and cultural activities. The legacy of Viking artistry lives on as a testomony to the complex interplay among creativity, lifestyle, and craftsmanship. The enduring appeal of Viking artwork lies in its ability to provide insights into the splendor, complexity, and rich cultural tapestry of the Viking Age, making sure that their innovative ancient past remains alive and colourful within the modern-day international.

Chapter 7: Conversion To Christianity

The transition from pagan beliefs to Christianity marked a profound and transformative length in Viking facts. The Vikings, recognized for his or her seafaring prowess and warrior way of existence, encountered a ultra-modern faith that would reshape their spiritual practices, cultural identity, and interactions with neighboring societies.

The way of conversion to Christianity modified into multifaceted, stimulated via the use of a complicated interplay of political, social, and non secular elements. The Vikings' interactions with Christian agencies, each through trade and conquest, exposed them to new mind and ideals. Additionally, the attraction of Christian buying and selling companions, diplomatic alliances, and cultural exchanges contributed to the sluggish embody of the trendy faith.

One of the pivotal moments within the conversion of the Vikings was the reign of King Olaf Tryggvason of Norway in the late 10th century. Olaf's efforts to sell Christianity blanketed the use of a combination of persuasion, international relations, and stress. His reign witnessed the development of churches, the appointment of Christian bishops, and the hooked up order of a Christian prison framework. These measures laid the inspiration for the combination of Christianity into Viking society.

The conversion of the Vikings changed into regularly a gradual technique that took place over generations. Families and corporations ought to adopt the brand new faith at their very very personal pace, and the transition have become often marked via way of a syncretic blending of pagan and Christian traditions. This allowed for a degree of continuity in cultural practices at the same time as accommodating the extremely-modern-day non secular ideals.

Missionaries done a massive position in the conversion manner. Christian missionaries, regularly despatched from Christian kingdoms in Europe, arrived in Viking territories to unfold the classes of Christianity. The artwork of missionaries like Ansgar, who's frequently called the "Apostle to the North," contributed to the dissemination of Christian thoughts and the popularity quo of Christian agencies.

The conversion of Scandinavia have become a complicated project that numerous across regions. While Norway noticed a reasonably speedy embody of Christianity, exclusive areas like Sweden and Denmark skilled a extra gradual shift.

The conversion of Iceland, as an example, have become encouraged through each political factors and the choice for cultural and diplomatic ties with Christian Europe.

The adoption of Christianity introduced about large changes in Viking spiritual practices and cultural expressions. Pagan rituals and deities steadily receded, replaced through way of Christian worship and the veneration of saints. The Christian calendar, fairs, and religious observances supplanted pagan traditions, reshaping the cultural landscape.

Art and structure furthermore contemplated the Vikings' encompass of Christianity. Pagan symbols and motifs have been step by step changed through Christian iconography inside the format of church buildings, sculptures, and artifacts. The evolution of Viking artistry pondered the wider shift in spiritual values and cultural expressions.

The conversion to Christianity moreover impacted Viking burial practices. Ship burials and grave goods, as soon as vital to Viking funerary customs, underwent adjustments as Christianity brought new beliefs about the afterlife and the remedy of the deceased. Christian burials frequently emphasised simplicity and non secular purity.

The conversion to Christianity had a long manner-achieving effects past the Viking homelands. As Vikings engaged in trade, raids, and exploration across Europe and past, they carried their newfound religion with them. The conversion allowed for cultural integration, diplomatic interactions, and religious syncretism that enriched the style of societies encountered with the resource of the Vikings.

In give up, the conversion of the Vikings to Christianity turn out to be a complex and multifaceted device that reshaped the course of Viking facts. The include of a cutting-edge faith, with its theological ideals, moral teachings, and cultural implications, marked a profound transformation in Viking society. The synthesis of pagan and Christian elements, the paintings of missionaries, and the gradual shift in cultural practices are all vital additives of the Vikings' transition to Christianity. This conversion left an indelible mark on the Viking Age, shaping the narratives of the beyond and influencing the cultural tapestry of the prevailing.

Exploration of North America

The Viking spirit of exploration and adventure prolonged beyond their European homelands to remote beaches, on the facet of the seashores of North America. The Viking exploration of North America stands as a first-rate achievement in maritime information, revealing the Vikings' navigational prowess, ambitious spirit, and their impact at the continent's history.

The Norse sagas, historic texts that blend statistics and mythology, provide insights into the Vikings' ventures to North America. The sagas point out a land called "Vinland," believed to be placed alongside the northeastern coast of North America. It is in the ones sagas that we discover money owed of the Vikings' exploration of a contemporary-day and unknown land.

The most well-known of those sagas is the "Saga of the Greenlanders," which recounts the story of Leif Erikson's adventure to Vinland across the yr 1000. Leif Erikson, son of the Norse explorer Erik the Red, is often credited with being one of the first Europeans to set foot on North American soil. The saga describes Vinland as an area with fertile land, slight weather, and sufficient property.

The archaeological evidence for Viking presence in North America emerge as determined within the 1960s at L'Anse aux Meadows, a internet site at the northern tip of Newfoundland, Canada. Excavations located out the stays of Viking homes, hearths, and artifacts, confirming the historical accuracy of the sagas and presenting tangible proof of Norse exploration in North America.

The L'Anse aux Meadows internet site online protected proof of ironworking, woodworking, and deliver repair, showcasing the Vikings' functionality to establish brief settlements and have interaction in numerous sports whilst in the New World. The internet web site on-line's region, with its proximity to wealthy fishing grounds and herbal assets, aligns with the descriptions of Vinland's favorable situations.

Viking exploration in North America prolonged past L'Anse aux Meadows. The sagas describe in addition expeditions to Vinland, with money owed of interactions the various Norse and indigenous peoples. The Vikings cited the indigenous human beings they encountered as "Skraelings," in all likelihood concerning severa Native American businesses. These interactions, documented inside the sagas, provide glimpses into the cultural exchanges and challenges the Vikings confronted on this new land.

The reasons inside the back of the Vikings' exploration of North America are multifaceted. Some theories advise that the Vikings were advocated via a choice to installation new trade routes, acquire treasured assets, and are trying to find fertile land. The sagas moreover thing out clashes with indigenous populations, highlighting the complexities of skip-cultural interactions in a land formerly unknown to the Vikings.

Despite their explorations, the Vikings' presence in North America did now not purpose eternal settlements or lasting colonization. The traumatic conditions posed with the aid of the sudden surroundings, limited assets, and interactions with indigenous agencies probable contributed to the Vikings' eventual departure from Vinland.

The Viking exploration of North America left a protracted-lasting legacy. It challenged prevailing ancient narratives that had lengthy held that Columbus have become the primary European to benefit the continent. The discovery of the L'Anse aux Meadows net internet site on line and the validation of the sagas' money owed broadened our information of early European exploration and their interactions with indigenous populations.

In modern-day instances, the exploration of North America thru the Vikings continues to captivate the imagination. Museums, educational packages, and scholarly research shed moderate in this wonderful bankruptcy in data. The Vikings' trips to North America function a testament to their spirit of adventure, their navigational competencies, and their ability to traverse sizeable distances in pursuit of recent horizons.

In forestall, the Viking exploration of North America represents a remarkable success in maritime records. The sagas' bills and the archaeological evidence at L'Anse aux Meadows offer a glimpse into the Vikings' journeys to a brand new and atypical land. Their presence in North America, but quick, serves as a testomony to their navigational prowess, cultural interest, and their indelible mark at the historical narratives of the continent.

Law and Justice in Viking Society

Within the dynamic tapestry of Viking society, the necessities of regulation and justice wove a complicated framework that dominated interactions, resolved disputes, and upheld social order. The

Vikings, said for his or her warrior ethos and seafaring expeditions, hooked up a system of criminal tips and felony practices that pondered their cultural values, social shape, and the want for balance.

Viking law modified right into a decentralized tool that numerous throughout one-of-a-type areas and agencies. The absence of a centralized authority meant that each location had its very personal laws and commonplace practices, regularly reflecting the unique desires and instances of the neighborhood populace. These prison recommendations had been upheld thru the mixed efforts of chieftains, network leaders, and assemblies.

A distinguished thing of Viking regulation became the idea of "Thing," a meeting or assembly in which prison topics were addressed, disputes have been settled, and choices were made. The Thing served as a democratic discussion board where unfastened men (and from time to time women) want to voice their opinions, gift proof, and make contributions to the device of justice. The Thing turn out to be a cornerstone of Viking governance, embodying requirements of network involvement and consensus-building.

In the absence of a formal crook code, Viking regulation relied intently on oral manner of life and the recitation of felony tips by way of using the use of human beings called "lawspeakers." These lawspeakers have been responsible for memorizing and reciting crook pronouncements within the path of Things, making sure that the network had get entry to to the legal hints and understood their implications.

One of the good sized contributions of Viking law end up its emphasis on reimbursement and restitution as a technique of resolving disputes. The idea of "weregild," moreover referred to as "guy-price," changed into essential to this method. Weregild changed right into a gadget wherein monetary repayment modified into paid to the sufferer or the victim's family in times of damage, theft, or murder. This device aimed to restore stability and prevent cycles of revenge.

Viking law moreover recognized superb social classes and mounted diverse outcomes primarily based absolutely totally on an man or woman's fame. Free men were afforded extra prison safety and rights in comparison to slaves or thralls. Penalties for crimes in the direction of better-repute people have been often more excessive than the ones for offenses dedicated in opposition to lower-recognition individuals.

Trial with the aid of using fight, referred to as "Holmgang," have become some other prison workout that allowed people to settle disputes thru physical fight in location of a crook manner. The outcome of the fight become believed to be determined via the gods, serving as a form of divine justice. While trial with the useful resource of fight have become now not the primary approach of resolving disputes, it contemplated the Vikings' notion in the function of future and the supernatural in subjects of justice.

Viking regulation prolonged past the domestic sphere to embody troubles of trade, maritime sports, and interactions with foreign places societies. The Vikings' big trade networks required rules to manipulate commercial enterprise transactions, making sure honest alternate and preventing fraud. The legal guidelines of the ocean, referred to as "Maritime Law," addressed issues collectively with shipwrecks, salvage rights, and disputes between seafarers.

Religion and superstition additionally stimulated Viking jail practices. Oaths and sworn statements held full-size weight, frequently invoking the gods as witnesses. Breaking an oath or giving fake testimony changed into considered a intense offense that invited divine punishment.

They have an effect on of Viking regulation is apparent in ancient sources and sagas that recount prison complaints, disputes, and judgments. The sagas, at the same time as blending records and delusion, offer insights into the social norms, cultural values, and complex felony strategies of Viking society.

In contemporary-day times, the legacy of Viking regulation keeps to captivate college students, historians, and fanatics. The take a look at of Viking prison practices sheds light on the complexities of their society, their approach to struggle choice, and their records of justice. Museums, academic research, and reenactments provide glimpses into the prison intricacies that dominated Viking companies and contribute to a deeper knowledge in their societal dynamics.

In end, regulation and justice in Viking society fashioned a vital framework that upheld order, resolved disputes, and maintained social harmony. The decentralized nature of Viking law, the democratic requirements of the Thing, and the emphasis on compensation and restitution mirror the Vikings' dedication to sincere governance and network involvement. Viking jail practices, at the same time as numerous and place-unique, left an indelible mark at the historical narratives of the Viking Age, enriching our expertise in their complicated cultural and social cloth.

Chapter 8: Viking Trade Routes And Exotic Goods

In the complicated internet of Viking way of lifestyles, trade emerged as a crucial thread that connected faraway lands, facilitated cultural exchange, and enriched the cloth and intellectual lives of Viking groups. The Vikings, renowned for their seafaring prowess and spirit of journey, launched into enormous alternate routes that spanned throughout Europe and past, bringing with them a treasure trove of one in all a type items and fostering connections that everyday their society.

The geographical format of Scandinavia, with its complex network of fjords, rivers, and coastal regions, facilitated the Vikings' improvement of superior shipbuilding strategies. The iconic Viking longships, characterised through manner of their easy layout and shallow drafts, were bendy vessels that allowed the Vikings to navigate every open seas and inland waterways effortlessly. These ships served because the conduits of trade, sporting precious cargo and forging connections with remote lands.

The Vikings' trade routes have been severa and an extended way-engaging in, spanning at some point of each maritime and overland routes. The Vikings ventured to the British Isles, the Baltic Sea, Russia, the Mediterranean, and on the equal time as far as the Middle East. Their presence in those regions became not simply approximately trade; it modified into a dynamic interplay that brought on the alternate of products, thoughts, and cultural practices.

One of the crucial element exchange routes that the Vikings navigated modified into the Baltic Sea. The area's enough sources, which encompass amber, furs, and timber, attracted Viking traders who exchanged the ones commodities for silver, costly objects, and outstanding gadgets from first rate factors of Europe. The Vikings' presence inside the Baltic moreover facilitated interactions with the Slavic peoples and contributed to the dissemination of cultural impacts.

The Vikings' exchange routes extended to the British Isles, in which they set up each non violent shopping for and promoting relationships and ambitious raiding expeditions. The Vikings' demand for English and Irish silver introduced about a extensive flow of overseas cash and goods among the Viking homelands and the British Isles. In cross returned, the Vikings introduced with them expensive gadgets, spices, textiles, and different superb gadgets that pondered their interactions with distant lands.

The Vikings' exploration and exchange routes furthermore led them to Russia and the Eastern European regions. The Volga change direction, connecting the Baltic Sea to the Black Sea, became a key artery that facilitated the trade of products among Viking consumers and the Byzantine Empire. Viking buyers brought furs, honey, and slaves from the north, whilst they acquired high priced items, silks, spices, and precious metals from the south.

The Vikings' engagement with the Middle East is evidenced via the presence of Islamic coins, textiles, and artifacts found in Viking archaeological web sites. These gadgets feature a tangible testament to the a protracted way-attaining change networks that related Viking traders with the Islamic global, especially thru intermediaries which incorporates the Rus traders in the East.

Exotic gadgets obtained via Viking trade routes executed a pivotal characteristic in shaping Viking society. The presence of highly-priced devices, which incorporates silks, spices, and jewelry, no longer handiest extended the recognition of individuals who possessed them but additionally enriched the material manner of lifestyles of Viking agencies. These devices, often showcased in burials and hoards, replicate the interconnectedness of Viking tradition with the broader international.

The Vikings' buying and selling activities had been no longer limited to bodily objects on my own; furthermore they engaged in the exchange of thoughts, spiritual ideals, and cultural practices.

The contact with one-of-a-kind cultures thru change routes stimulated the development of Viking artwork, language, and non secular ideals. The adoption of distant places factors into Viking manner of life is apparent in the ingenious motifs, area names, and even in the sagas that recount the Vikings' exploits.

In modern instances, the legacy of Viking change routes continues to captivate pupils and fanatics alike. Archaeological discoveries, historic facts, and museum exhibitions provide insights into the complexities of Viking alternate networks and the severa array of products that flowed through their palms. The Viking Age stands as a testomony to the some distance-engaging in effect of trade on shaping societies, fostering connections, and shaping the fabric and cultural history of communities.

In closing, Viking trade routes and the change of excellent items stood as a colourful tapestry that interwove Viking society with the wider international. The a long way-reaching change networks, maritime exploits, and interactions with severa cultures enriched the Vikings' material lives and increased their horizons. The Vikings' alternate routes have been not pretty plenty commodities; they had been conduits of connection and cultural exchange that left an indelible mark on the historic narratives of the Viking Age.

Legacy of Viking Influence in Europe

The legacy of the Vikings' presence in Europe reverberates via the annals of records, leaving a long lasting effect on manner of lifestyles, language, governance, and the very fabric of societies they encountered. The Vikings' dynamic interactions, seafaring expeditions, and cultural exchanges led to a multifaceted legacy that continues to shape the European landscape to at the moment.

One of the maximum superb contributions of the Vikings is their have an effect on on language. The Norse language, Old Norse, left an indelible mark at the English language, especially via the incorporation of Norse terms and terms. Words like "sky," "egg," "leg," and "husband" are only a few examples of the linguistic legacy that the Vikings imparted to English. The blending of Norse and English languages stable a linguistic tapestry that enriched the vocabulary and expressions of the English-speakme global.

Viking have an effect on prolonged to the governance and criminal systems of the regions they encountered. The Vikings' emphasis on democratic practices, as exemplified by means of the use of the Thing, left an imprint at the improvement of nearby governance systems. The concepts of assembly-primarily based decision-making and network involvement advocated the evolution of European crook and political institutions.

The reputation quo of the Danelaw in England marked a massive duration of Viking have an impact on inside the area. The Danelaw, a region in England wherein Danish prison recommendations and customs prevailed, reflects the Vikings' capability to combine their personal prison and administrative structures into present societies. The legacy of the Danelaw can despite the fact that be seen inside the area names, prison practices, and cultural exchanges that emerged in the course of that generation.

Viking artistry, with its tough designs, motifs, and craftsmanship, left a protracted lasting legacy in European art work. The ornate carvings on church buildings, the interwoven styles in textiles, and the symbolism in jewelry all deliver echoes of Viking have an impact on. The fusion of Viking modern sensibilities with the winning innovative traditions of Europe led to a super aesthetic that continues to captivate modern-day-day audiences.

The Vikings' maritime prowess and navigational talents contributed to enhancements in shipbuilding and exploration. The upgrades in supply format, together with the enduring longships, stimulated the improvement of European shipbuilding techniques. The understanding of navigation, tides, and trade routes that the Vikings possessed contributed to the expansion of European exploration and maritime exchange.

The Vikings' effect on spiritual practices is also noteworthy. The conversion of the Vikings to Christianity introduced approximately a mixing of Christian beliefs with pre-existing pagan traditions. This syncretic method to religion delivered approximately the preservation of cultural practices and ideals on the identical time as integrating them into the framework of Christianity. This legacy is seen in present day-day Scandinavian spiritual customs and cultural celebrations.

The cultural alternate fostered through Viking exchange routes enriched European societies with a severa array of goods, thoughts, and perspectives. The Vikings' interactions with extraordinary cultures introduced foreign places factors into European societies, contributing to the wealthy tapestry of cultural variety that characterizes Europe in recent times.

In the sector of exploration, the Vikings' journeys to North America challenged winning historic narratives approximately European exploration. The Viking presence in North America, as evidenced by using using archaeological discoveries and sagas, reshaped our information of early touch between Europe and the New World. The legacy of their exploration keeps to persuade historical interpretations and discussions approximately early transatlantic connections.

The legacy of Viking effect in Europe is a testomony to the complex interplay among cultures, the enduring impact of exploration, and the dynamism of cultural exchange. The Vikings' imprint on language, artwork, governance, religion, and exploration serves as a reminder in their enduring characteristic in shaping the ancient narratives and cultural tapestry of Europe. In contemporary times, the fascination with Viking history, reenactments, museum exhibitions, and educational studies all mirror the iconic enchantment of the Vikings' legacy and their lasting effect at the European continent.

Chapter 9: Decline And Fragmentation

As the Viking Age advanced, the vigor and harmony that had described the early days of Viking growth began out to offer manner to a duration of decline and fragmentation. The elements contributing to this alteration were multifaceted, stemming from changing political dynamics, outside pressures, shifts in exchange routes, and internal divisions internal Viking society.

One of the factors that played a feature inside the decline of Viking power emerge as the emergence of more potent centralized states in Europe. As kingdoms like England, France, and Norway consolidated their energy and prolonged their territories, they posed greater disturbing conditions to Viking raiders and settlers. The once-strategic objectives of Viking raids have been now fortified and capable of mounting ambitious defenses.

Furthermore, the weakening of the Abbasid Caliphate and the decline of the Islamic worldwide's monetary and political stability disrupted the drift of valuable items along trade routes that the Vikings had previously exploited. This had an impact on Viking sports which includes change and plundering, reducing their get proper of get admission to to to the super items and wealth that had once fueled their expeditions.

Internal divisions inside Viking society also contributed to the decline. The vastness of Viking territories, blended with the absence of a centralized authority, introduced about rivalries and conflicts among exquisite Viking agencies. This inner fragmentation weakened their potential to mount cohesive army expeditions or maintain cohesion in the face of outside stressful situations.

The Christianization of Viking territories added about considerable modifications in social dynamics. The adoption of Christianity precipitated the decline of traditional pagan practices, and with it, a shift in the values and beliefs that had as quickly as caused Viking exploration and conquest. As Viking society transformed, so did their motivations and aspirations.

The geographical expansion of Viking sports additionally contributed to their decline. The massive distances included via manner of Viking expeditions, from Russia to North America, stretched their resources and made the logistics of maintaining a cohesive presence tough. This geographical unfold, coupled with the regulations of conversation and transportation, hindered the Vikings' capability to answer successfully to growing threats.

Climate modifications additionally played a position in the decline of Viking growth. The "Medieval Warm Period," characterised by using milder temperatures, needed to start with facilitated Viking exploration and colonization. However, because the climate shifted, harsher situations affected agricultural productiveness, change routes, and the sustainability of Viking settlements in marginal lands.

The decline of the Vikings is likewise associated with their slow integration into the societies they as quick as raided. Over time, Viking settlers assimilated into neighborhood populations, adopting their languages, customs, and approaches of lifestyles. This method of integration in addition eroded the super Viking identification and contributed to the dissolution in their as soon as-unified cultural and political the the front.

The final recorded Viking raid on England came about in 1066, even as King Harald Hardrada of Norway come to be defeated at the Battle of Stamford Bridge. This event marked a symbolic surrender to the technology of Viking raids and conquests. Shortly thereafter, the Norman Conquest of England led via manner of William the Conqueror marked a brand new bankruptcy in European records and signaled the decline of Viking sports activities.

In stop, the decline and fragmentation of the Vikings' have an effect on and activities were formed with the aid of using a aggregate of internal and outside factors. Changing political dynamics, more potent treasured states, shifts in exchange routes, the unfold of Christianity, internal rivalries, and climate adjustments all contributed to the decline of Viking energy. While the Viking Age had as speedy as been characterised with the useful resource of daring voyages and cultural exchanges, the factors said in this financial ruin heralded the realization of this dynamic duration and paved the way for the subsequent chapters in European statistics.

Archaeological Discoveries and Insights

Archaeology has completed a pivotal role in uncovering the hidden layers of Viking records, supplying a tangible window into the lives, customs, and accomplishments of these historic seafarers. Through meticulous excavation, assessment of artifacts, and the take a look at of burial web sites and settlements, archaeologists have unearthed a wealth of insights that beautify our information of the Viking Age.

One of the most iconic archaeological discoveries related to the Vikings is the Oseberg deliver burial in Norway. Discovered in 1904, the Oseberg deliver contained the remarkably preserved stays of women, at the side of a trove of tough artifacts, textiles, or maybe animals. This burial net site shed slight at the cultural and social practices of the Vikings, providing insights into their ideals, craftsmanship, and the jobs of ladies in Viking society.

Another big find is the Gokstad deliver burial, additionally in Norway. Dating to the 9th century, this burial contained a nicely-preserved Viking deliver and the remains of a person determined via way of his property. The Gokstad supply supplied valuable records approximately Viking shipbuilding techniques, alternate networks, and the social reputation of its occupant.

L'Anse aux Meadows, a domain at the northern tip of Newfoundland, Canada, stands as a testomony to Viking exploration in North America. Discovered inside the Sixties, this archaeological net internet site determined the remains of Viking homes, device, and artifacts, validating the sagas' payments of Norse presence in the New World. The discoveries at L'Anse aux Meadows have broadened our information of the volume of Viking exploration and their interactions with indigenous populations.

The discovery of the Jelling Stones in Denmark unveiled a rich supply of historic information. These runestones, erected within the tenth century via King Harald Bluetooth, provide inscriptions that provide insights into Viking political energy, religious beliefs, and the reputation quo of Christianity in Scandinavia.

The excavation of Viking settlements along with Birka in Sweden, Ribe in Denmark, and Dublin in Ireland has discovered out the format of Viking towns, the employer of exchange, and the each day lives of the population. These web sites offer a complete view of Viking town lifestyles, which include exchange practices, craft manufacturing, and social systems.

Viking supply burials, with their splendid reveals, offer a glimpse into the funerary rituals and ideals of the Vikings. Ship burials like the ones at Sutton Hoo in England and Borre in Norway contain every richly decorated artifacts and the remains of people, reflecting the Vikings' connection to the ocean and their belief in an afterlife.

The have a study of Viking hoards, on the facet of the Cuerdale Hoard in England and the Silverdale Hoard in Norway, has shed mild on the economic and exchange networks of the Vikings. These hoards, containing cash, jewelry, and treasured metals, spotlight the Vikings' participation in global trade and their accumulation of wealth.

Beyond the physical artifacts, archaeology has found out insights into Viking weight loss plan, fitness, and every day bodily sports through the analysis of skeletal stays. Isotopic assessment of enamel and bones has provided facts approximately the Vikings' migration patterns, weight loss plan versions, and publicity to particular environments.

Through advances in archaeological techniques which includes some distance off sensing, DNA assessment, and isotope evaluation, researchers keep to find out new dimensions of Viking records. Collaborations among archaeologists, historians, linguists, and extraordinary experts have delivered approximately extra nuanced understandings of Viking lifestyle, interactions, and contributions to global facts.

In give up, archaeological discoveries have illuminated the Viking Age with remarkable info, imparting insights into different factors in their lives. From supply burials to agreement excavations, the artifacts and insights unearthed through archaeologists offer a mosaic of the Vikings' achievements, beliefs, and interactions. These discoveries preserve to captivate the imagination of students and fanatics alike, enriching our facts of this dynamic and complicated historical generation.

Chapter 10: Revival Of Norse Culture

The legacy of the Vikings transcends the pages of records, as their manner of existence and ancient past have professional a first-rate resurgence in contemporary-day instances. The revival of Norse life-style, regularly referred to as the "Viking Revival," is a testament to the long-lasting fascination and impact of this historic civilization on modern-day society.

The revival of Norse manner of lifestyles gained momentum in the 19th century as college students, artists, and fanatics began to re-ignite hobby inside the Vikings' achievements, myths, and manner of lifestyles. The rediscovery of medieval Norse literature, collectively with the sagas and Eddas, fueled a renewed appreciation for Viking narratives and worldviews. These literary works provided a window into the cultural ethos, values, and ingenious universe of the Vikings.

The scenario of archaeology additionally finished a pivotal function in inspiring the revival. The discovery of Viking artifacts, burial web sites, and settlements furnished tangible connections to the past and ignited interest approximately the fabric culture of the Vikings. Museums and exhibitions showcasing those findings allowed the general public to have interaction with the physical remnants of Viking facts, fostering a deeper understanding and connection.

Artists and writers decided perception in Norse mythology, sagas, and imagery. Painters like John Bauer and Carl Larsson captured the epic and fantastical factors of Viking recollections in their artwork. Authors like J.R.R. Tolkien, prompted by way of using Norse myths, crafted tough myth worlds that resonated with scenario subjects from Viking literature.

The Viking Revival prolonged to language as well. In Iceland, the Old Norse language emerge as preserved, permitting the reading and know-how of historical texts. Furthermore, efforts were made to reconstruct and revive Old Norse for modern-day use, permitting fans to have interaction with the language of the sagas and be a part of greater intimately with Viking way of life.

The emergence of neo-pagan movements, frequently known as Heathenry or Ásatrú, marked a tremendous aspect of the Viking Revival. These present day pagan practices draw concept from Norse mythology and non secular ideals, searching out to reconstruct and adapt the non secular traditions of the Vikings. Ásatrúarfélagið, based totally in Iceland in 1972, is an example of a recognized Ásatrú company that fosters a present day interpretation of Norse spirituality.

Viking reenactment groups and historical societies have flourished, allowing lovers to step all over again in time and revel in elements of Viking lifestyles firsthand. These corporations engage in sports activities which encompass conventional crafts, re-growing battles, and adopting duration clothing to immerse themselves inside the every day workout routines and worrying conditions confronted thru the Vikings.

The impact of the Viking Revival extends to popular manner of lifestyles. From blockbuster movies like "Thor" and "Vikings" to video games like "Assassin's Creed: Valhalla," the Vikings have captured the imagination of world audiences. These portrayals, even as frequently a mixture of facts and fantasy, make contributions to the popular fascination with Viking manner of existence.

Tourism has additionally capitalized on the appeal of the Vikings. Sites with historic Viking importance, collectively with Jelling in Denmark and L'Anse aux Meadows in Canada, appeal to visitors eager to revel in the sector of the Vikings firsthand. Viking-themed activities, gala's, and markets provide opportunities to immerse oneself within the environment of the Viking Age.

In conclusion, the revival of Norse tradition is a multifaceted phenomenon that encompasses literature, paintings, language, spirituality, reenactment, and famous subculture. The enduring enchantment of the Vikings' achievements, sagas, and mystique has stimulated individuals and groups spherical the area to have interaction with and make contributions to the safety and reinterpretation of this wealthy cultural background. The Viking Revival stands as a testomony to the timelessness of the Vikings' legacy and their enduring impact on our current worldwide.

The Enduring Mystique of the Vikings

The Vikings, with their seafaring expeditions, sagas of heroism, and complicated cultural tapestry, preserve to captivate the creativeness and intrigue people spherical the arena. The enchantment of the Vikings lies now not pleasant in their ancient importance but additionally within the layers of thriller, exploration, and resilience that represent their legacy.

One of the elements contributing to the enduring mystique of the Vikings is the enigmatic nature of their history. While historians and archaeologists have pieced together large insights, there are despite the fact that gaps in our data of sure factors of Viking lifestyle and sports activities. This ambiguity invites hypothesis and fosters an air of thriller that beckons researchers and fanatics to delve deeper into the unknown.

The Vikings' exploits are often tinged with factors of journey and hazard, including to their mystique. The image of Viking longships sailing during treacherous seas, ambitious raids on far off beaches, and fearless warriors struggling with forces past their control evokes a experience of formidable that resonates with the human fascination for exploration and the unknown.

The Viking sagas, with their combination of history and myth, contribute to the mystique surrounding the Vikings. These epic recollections, often full of gods, monsters, and supernatural feats, cross beyond time and region, presenting a window into the mindset of the Vikings and the imaginitive global they inhabited. The interaction among history and fiction in the sagas gives layers of complexity to the Vikings' legacy.

The rich symbolism and complex craftsmanship of Viking artifacts upload to their air of mystery of mystique. The ornate designs, runic inscriptions, and interwoven motifs located on jewelry, weapons, and normal objects reflect the Vikings' self-control to aesthetics and their capability to carry which means thru paintings. The symbolism inner those artifacts invitations interpretations that bridge the distance the various past and the triumphing.

The Vikings' particular non secular ideals and cosmology make a contribution to their mystique. The gods of Norse mythology, together with Odin, Thor, and Loki, offer a glimpse into the Vikings' religious global and the forces they believed formed their lives. The complicated relationships among gods, humans, and the herbal world add an element of complexity that maintains to intrigue scholars and lovers alike.

The stark assessment the various Vikings' dual identity as raiders and traders fuels their mystique. The Vikings had been no longer truely marauders; they have been moreover expert navigators, consumers, and settlers who established connections with distant lands. This duality worrying conditions traditional narratives and underscores the complexity in their cultural and historic roles.

The Viking Age's resonance with venture subjects of courage, resilience, and survival gives to their mystique. The Vikings faced harsh landscapes, extreme climate, and adversities that demanded resourcefulness and determination. This narrative of overcome worrying conditions resonates with humans searching for notion of their private lives.

The legacy of the Vikings' have an effect on on language, artwork, governance, exploration, and change networks contributes to their enduring mystique. The impact of the Vikings transcends time, as their contributions maintain to shape contemporary-day societies and cultural narratives. This bridge among the past and the prevailing fuels our fascination with the Vikings and the perception that their legacy isn't limited to the pages of statistics however remains an crucial a part of our modern-day international.

In the location of famous lifestyle, the Vikings' mystique thrives. From literature to movie, tv to video games, the Vikings' presence stays amazing. The air of mystery of adventure, mystery, and large-than-lifestyles personas depicted in those mediums perpetuates the fascination with the Vikings and keeps their legacy alive inside the collective attention.

In end, the enduring mystique of the Vikings stems from the mixture of historic significance, enigmatic elements, and their multifaceted cultural contributions. The attraction of their information, sagas, artifacts, and symbolism attracts humans of numerous backgrounds into the orbit of the Viking Age. The Vikings' legacy serves as a timeless reminder that under the layers of information lies a charming tapestry that maintains to encourage and captivate, connecting us to a global of adventure, exploration, and the unknown.

www.ingramcontent.com/pod-product-compliance
Lightning Source LLC
Chambersburg PA
CBHW070737020526
44118CB00035B/1454